Dancing in the Tabernacle

Dancing in the Tabernacle

TRACI L. SLATTON

parvati
press

Published in 2011 by Parvati Press
parvatipress.com

Copyright © 2011 by Traci L. Slatton

No part of this book may be reproduced or used, stored in any information retrieval system or transmitted in any form or by any means, electronic, mechanical, photocopying, recording, or otherwise, without prior written permission from Parvati Press, except in the case of brief quotations embodied in critical articles and reviews.

Cover and text design and composition by
Drew Stevens, studiodrew.net

Cover photos by Alexandra Czernin-Spencer

ISBN 978-0-9846726-1-5

Library of Congress Control Number: 2011941299

CONTENTS

ATZILUT & ASIYAH   1
ONE WEEKEND IN THE ASTRAL PLANE   2
SECOND SIGHT   3
HEALING HANDS   4
DASKALOS   6
SPIRIT HOUSES   8
TROPIC OF NEPTUNE   9
THE DREAM, HENRI ROUSSEAU, 1910   10
THE CATHEDRAL   12
PERSEPHONE   14
TIKKUN OLAM   16
MY CHILDREN'S ARMS   18
CHIROMANCY   19
THE TAXI DRIVER   20
GAYATRI MANTRA   21
VALLEY OF THE BUTTERFLIES, PETALOUDES, PAROS   22
TIGER IN THE GARDEN   24
ICE PACKS   26
SWEET MOTHER   27
MY DADDY'S THUMB   28
DECONSTRUCTING THE ASTROLOGY OF LOVE   30
PUTS & CALLS   31
ORACLE   32
VIRGIN   34
PONN FARR   36
ICON   38
PAGAN   39
ARTIST   40
IN ITALY, MANNEQUINS HAVE NIPPLES   41
TRIPTYCH PLUS ONE, AFTER RUMI   42
THE ARTHUR MURRAY LOVER   44

THE SECRET, WILLIAM BOUGUEREAU, 1875	45
CRUCIFEROUS VEGETABLES	46
DOMESTICATED BEASTS	47
REVELATIONS	48
HEAVEN'S GATE	50
BLUES, GRAYS & BIG-HEAD WHITES	52
THE KAMA SUTRA/TORAH	54
STORIES FOR VLADIMIR	56
GANESHA	58
THE BEAR MAN	60
REFLECTIONS FROM THE TWELFTH HOUSE	61
BATHSHEBA	62
KING LEAR	63
THE CATHEDRAL AT COLOGNE	64
THE ROAD AFTER DAMASCUS	66
PRAYER	68
BODY & PSALM	70
THE ECLECTIC AGNOSTIC	71
IN MY NEXT LIFETIME	72
SEVA	74

Acknowledgments 76

*In loving memoriam to Granny Bee,
Lorine Birdie Barnum Adkerson,
whose light is with me always*

ATZILUT & ASIYAH

they are the twin snakes coiling
around the root that rises
from the foundation of everything
the ice-blown mountain and the luscious valley
the North and the South Poles
East where the sun ascends and West
where it sets, where hope goes
when the soul sleeps from its jubilant travail
through the flesh
blazing red-orange corona and indigo shadow
they are the twin irises of God's two eyes

during the day I wander
watching people in the street
they walk in a mania of flickering light
rainbow envelopes and gold serpents crawling
exulting germinating in their bodies I wonder
Are they awake?
Am I?

at night the tabernacle opens
and I succumb to the dance
wedging myself into the waltz
between heaven and hell
when I am not dancing I am praying
when prayer fails the gate opens
and I am broken and whole
falling into two places at once

ONE WEEKEND IN THE ASTRAL PLANE

On Fridays there are owls in your room
   with eyes like blisters they fly out of cypress dormers
   that weren't there the day before
   and painted walls dissolve into paper
   flowers and violin waltzes drift out from Victorian times
   and your feet burn and your knees quiver
   and your legs can't contain the saltfire

On the Sabbath the angels come to sing
   and light scrims through the air, platinum
   globules and Glory to the Creator
   you can't sit and read because they tug
   at your sleeve and breeze through your hair
   and your heart wells up and you sigh
   and you cry and finally you give over
   and kneel in the shadows and bite your tongue
   through 'til it spills milk and honey

On Sunday rest is blue, cobalt blue and cerulean blue
   the color of lakes in Atlantis and laser beams
   from the Pleiades and of bell flowers by dirt roads
   that lead past ruined temples
   the blue stands in rows like webs on parade
   and from these like urns or amphorae of holy water
   a net is woven to carry the rest of the week
   to hold in your hands the ferment of heaven

SECOND SIGHT

"I see dead people."
　　　　　The Sixth Sense

Clairvoyance is a remorseless gift,
Fit only for the damned.
They ought to have a dedicated circle of hell
Specially for it. I didn't ask to see the colors swirling about
Bodies like silks in the crazy bazaar of the human
Condition, or the angels singing like a chorus
In the theater of the absurd.

Every time I laid hands on Ruth,
Azrael, too gorgeous like the sun
To behold, whispered, she will die. Leukemia
Got her. My nephew succumbed;
He was three years old. No living body
Is dearer than that of a child to the one
Who can see the soul, that sacred container
Of the flesh, leaking out around it.
I have estranged from those who should
Be dearest. They do not speak my language
Of subtle bodies, they do not hear the voices
Raised in hymns, they barely inhabit the same Earth
As me, so pierced through with heaven as it is.

Did I know in advance
When I saw the eight-pointed star
Kissing the crown of a little boy's head?
Could I have done anything about it?
To preempt the Angel of Death
Is more than illusion, in the throes
Of transcendental bliss, and less than
Possible, in fact prohibited, by the consensual
Orb of our humanity, marbled through with light though it is.

Satori isn't all it's cracked up to be.

HEALING HANDS

Some days I the healer see ill clients
back-to-back, one hour fifteen
minutes allotted to each
though I set a boundary at one
hour for the session. Boundaries
like all the figures of life efface. At some point
a young woman with breast
cancer trudges in and my heart
swells, a container of twigs
and peeling bark holding her grief
with my unrelated sorrows like sap that circulates
after the frost, and the shape
of my hands blurs before my eyes
until they are mechanistic factotums
used in my life like a disease
to slap a dog, to shatter
my former husband's glasses on his face—how not
to be enlightened—three
stitches on his brow, long ago
before we were married
when I discovered photographs
of him with another
woman. He has a new love now, younger than I,
blond. Every passage
of atonement
requires mourning, and mourning
leaves behind
an empty vessel. There's no
other way but slowly to fill the self
with the self, and tenderly. So I hand
myself over to the oblivion

at the center of the human torus
drawing my clients in with me
praising god the Artist
and obliterator of all
on those busy days
when bodies like hours fall away
and I stand first
in my own hollowness
and simultaneously
in the stricken blankness within another.

DASKALOS

"Faith is a blush before God."
Rabbi Abraham Heschel

She is a shambling figure, hunched
at that joint where the vertebrae ply into the sacrum,
bald from the chemotherapy.

In her aura I see the flowers
with which she refuses
to adorn herself, this singular accountant
with parents who visit her, their only child,
through the spirit cords that spill easily
between realms of body and psalm.

He is an old Greek man, a magus from heaven. Death
has not dimmed his light. He is holy
as only one immersed in the Christic
whether Jew, Hindu, or Agnostic,
can finally embody, egregious
as we all are who have ever taken on flesh
even for that profoundest purpose
of praising God. His healer's hands
like a dove's wings
touch now only through spirit,
though some husk of the authoritarian personality lingers
with the soul spore freed from its fragile casing.

His supervision lends a mending
where my own skill falls short.
I have learned the hard way
healing is not curing
but I still, polarized with sin, seek the end to pain.
He is subtler than I.
He pulls down a pyramid of light
informs her etheric body with a shining alabaster river
lets it seep down through those stones

and branches the body's bones.
He invites in the archangels.
I am awash in awe but I am not now blushing
in this moment I have no faith
that sentiment of separation
there is only knowing
I am not coy with God
our familiarity has made us comrades
partners, equals.

In the end there is mystery. They two depart.
With the affectionate and embarrassed
ceremony of the living, she opens a door
to an exit hallway
and closes it on his frank and diaphanous appraisal
of my work. Whatever my passion
in the incendiary transfigured moment
Now I redden, fruitfully aware
of good
and evil, my own shortcomings
as a healer
and a Jew
a mother, a wife, a woman.
Go back within, he tells me,
keep working within
keep praying
research truth.

Then there is silence
like lilacs after the rain,
lavender and white
blossoms that she will not be
wearing next week
without the miracle
Daskalos and God
and pale, faithless I
hold forth for her
to choose.

SPIRIT HOUSES

Bangkok, January 1

The Thai are the prettiest of peoples. Glowing amber skin
And sloe eyes, a perpetual smile and certain
Grace. They season their fresh foods with lemon grass,
Peppers, ginger, and lime. At the Floating Market, slender-limbed
Women sell whole or fried bananas, sweet Asian bananas no longer
Than my hand, from the semilunar bone to the tip
Of a third phalange. We tourists are kept happy:
Elephant rides and elaborate dances for a hundred baht;
At the Thon Buri snake farm, a clowning man offers his head
To a crocodile's mouth, elicits a roar of laughter; the little girls
Of Patpong open their lips, discrete hospitality
To grinning foreign businessmen, and send
Their money home. Saffron-robed monks chant
In a thousand watts; their voices rise like eclipsed
Angels in the city. Klongs
Slide under wood shacks, stilts like delicate fingers
Walking on the water, and sometimes an unhurried Thai
Can be spotted carrying flowers, adorning with a tender
Hand the tiny, gilded temple—the gorgeous house
Outside each hut—every family provides
For the teeming spirits of the land. *Mai pen rye*, don't worry,
God disposes. So it is that the hospitable
So freely spiritualized
Belong with bodies of such beauty.

TROPIC OF NEPTUNE

Hypnogogic, I wander to the water's edge
A voice summons me, tunneling
   a rhythmic rope threading through a vanishing tube

I am wearing a filmy white dress. An island, green and rocky,
Seen in another life
Awaits. I am leaving behind
A wedding party, someone else's. I expect dolphins, they don't come
I am barefoot upon tawny pebbles
   commit to the ocean

In the dream I am awake
I am not afraid. It is the time to hear voices
This coital passage of the Lord of Prophecy and Seas
   ask a question
Of this master's voice. Urgent and dire, I ask
Knowing I will not remember
The secret to possessing my love
To creation itself, when I open
My eyes my hands will be empty
They have gripped a vapor
or a wave

I reach the island and climb. The voice falls silent.
The form of my beloved appears in the confusion
Our conversation ebbs before awareness can be consummated
   bereft, before I have been not alone

The next hundred unnumbered nights
   waiting
For one intonation, for the sussurus
Through the hollow core of my being
That signals a Presence
Firmament merging into the waters

THE DREAM, HENRI ROUSSEAU, 1910

She reclines on a matte red sofa
outstretched hand pointing to the striped sarong
covering the polite idea of a pelvis
of a native woman making music.
I am not tempted to hear it
except in theory. Two lions:
one affronts with his eyes of chartreuse
circles and hollow irises. There are birds,
not singing, flowers—blue, blush—unscented,
and rubbery orange fruits like ornaments
tied to a stylized tree. One monkey
laughs at the full moon, a disembodied sound,
daylight waning but not compliant,
not passionate enough to surrender, not yet. The elephant's
eye beckons,
numb memory and abstract wisdom, his trunk
erect. A dream, but she is not asleep.
She is looking with one Egyptian eye.
Dark tresses toy with a rosy aureole
that not even a loner in a trench coat
sitting in one of those smoky loud titty bars
would want to touch. Her hip is turned
to conceal her fruitful center, the curve
of thigh rounding into chaste knees
and crossed ankles. Her body is lighter
than the moon, her breasts, stretched
like balloons on a ribbon of light
in this insensate tableau of the unconscious.
The garden of my mind is not so untouchable
I hope. But I, like the Christ in Gethsemane,
am vulnerable to my own doubts.

The velvety force within may be betrayed
or tempted by the worldly part of me
into an impermeable surface
an apostate primitivism where only what is seen
carries meaning.
I pray to escape a tactile-deprivation hell
of my own making. I affirm my imperfection.
This vessel has cracks
for the light to pour through:
I dream of touching God.

THE CATHEDRAL

She has night-time hair and she flirts
with boys too young like green peaches
that can be licked but not bit

In the transept lives a homeless woman
in another century she would have begged alms
sold matches but time that old wit has tickled
her brain and she understands now

    She would rather dawdle in the sun with lazy
    loose limbs playing cat's cradle with red yarn
    in profligate fingers but she works every day

In the nave sit the congregants, voices soprano
some tenor or darker, they all shout advice
the men in black coats bray things the Father once said
the women all want to be fed

    She eats gruel and licks the cream
    out of pastry shells, a hundred leaves with nectar
    for her tongue and her lips under closed eyes

In the apse the Priest swings the dreams, myrrh
and sandalwood smoke wreathes against trefoil windows
crinkled with Madonna Mary's golding hair and crimson
blood of passion and white curls of the Lord's flock

    She tells stories that are lies and truths
    they peek out like rosy toes from her sheets
    that are threadbare with purple silk
    and her throat ripples with laughter

But the spire, the spire rises, so bidden all eyes lift
to the sun and the unforgiving moon, indulgence and gloom
on days when heaven drops down the clouds caress it
and the flood strikes the soot from the facade

    She rolls onto her soft belly humming psalms
    and forgotten hymns, the intent is holy
    and they are stones smooth and heavy from the deep
    earth's veins that multiply atop one another
    to build this structure of worship, the living Sanctum

PERSEPHONE

they do not understand
I go willingly
there, through the purple
petals
down the yellow stamen
dusting my chiton with saffron,
descending green stalks,
coursing down through bulbous
ochre roots into the dim
spaces, deficient places
where shades weep
the shadow's keep
the spirits' sweep
of unrequited love

it was never rape
I blossomed them
took fees for my services
from under their tongues
a drachma or two
on their lids
nursed their dulled wounds
recovered their swoons
made song in the ruins
of their hearth-bound
hymns

a blessing, a service
polishing bone
whispering to stone
to those diffused creatures

no longer growing
no longer glowing
in their final keep knowing
they are wisps unravelling
the weave of Lachesis
in the loom of time

I am free to go
my juices scattered below
the mysteries revived
the spirits survived
to rejoin the mother
the sun and the vine
the stalk and the ear
another fruitful year
drawing new seeds near
from husks of the old
rising up through the roots
through the sticky stem
and the fiery bloom
to the pomegranate
fruits, crimson and sad
live and then mourn
the contract is born
in the agora of form
with each new birth on the flowering
earth

TIKKUN OLAM

In the evenings, I meditate.
This after bathing my daughters
washing their long soft hair
with a flowery emulcent shampoo
selecting with them tomorrow's pleated
skirts from out of jumbled closets
sharing a bright fairy tale bedtime book
or two, if I yield to their pleas, lying
with each individually
first in the lavender room
with the spinning Buddhist prayer lantern
that is my little daughter's
then in my eldest's cozy red room
whose window looks out onto a cityscape
silhouetted against the lush pointillism of night
after walking the dog
scrubbing her splattered bowl, replenishing
it with the scientifically designed
trademark food that enhances the sheen
of her shaggy Westie coat
after filing a sheaf of unruly correspondence
returning calls
scribbling a list for the next day's marketing
picking up the day's objects strewn
like restive thoughts around
the sacred kinetic spaces
in which we live.
Is there a moment when I am not
repairing the world?

I am well aware that God
that Untidy Mistress
creates it all.
    This incremental
holographic atonement
of countless domestic gestures
consecrates the entirety
as the ocean is resplendent
in its every salty drop.
It is entropy that recedes
like any surrendered samsara
behind the centripetal prayers
of my hands that care for
children, animals, love's artifacts.

My heart, untroubled, visits
the many mansions of the Lord
some post mezzuzim
others sport lares
they are all homes with unmade beds
unswept floors and young eyes
shining with unshed tears
for distant princesses
and for the tidy childhood blessings
of wishing stars
that enlighten the chaos of heaven.

MY CHILDREN'S ARMS

for my daughters

In my children's arms, round like hula hoops
there is fizz redelicious of my quarnicky heart
all gooped over with toockly cooties and broken
from having stepped on the cracks
                of my mother's back

In my children's bellies, soft like banana dough
there are spangles all bubbly set in my sloop eyes
and rainbow gurgles that clummer hum in my throat
from songs that were shuckle shushed too long ago
                by those who should know

On my children's heads, crunchy sweet and true
there are tickle stars growing from flowergold sleeves
knit about with fairykin pumpkins and leprechaun lofts
and glimmer charm wags that my soul lost on its way
                from heaven to stay

In my children's arms, in my children's eyes
there is love and anguish and knowing too wise
for this piddledunk world and its spinachy ways
its clambersome nights and blistering days
I offer my arms for their snuggletug ease
    for their dream down wares and their 'zactly stuff, please
God
                let it be enough

CHIROMANCY

for Naomi

In her hands I see the shape of the woman
my daughter will be. Her palms are square
like mine, soft lines crisscrossing a pink
field, like the grid of love and separation
that life engraves
upon a heart.
Big hands for a child, and she'll be tall,
shapely, chestnut hair framing an oval face
that recalls mine, only prettier,
all divined in that lush and prominent
mount at the base of the thumb.
High cheekbones and a mouth that smiles
readily, pouts and plays, sings
nonsense rhymes in the made-up language
of her imaginary sisters Lassa and Carinna Snid.
It's all bespoke in her wide strong fingers, the sturdy
tools some peasant ancestor bequeathed us both.
Now in these silly months between five and a quarter
and five and a half, I can close my hand around her fist
and feel the pulse of her, the passion
and the mischief, all her tender flesh
in its exquisite incompletion. I have treasured her
littleness. It keeps her with me
where I can witness the precious measures
of her lifeline, every curve and indent
along its path. She skips beside me,
the woman she will be taking form
in the clasp we share. It becomes my prayer,
my mantra, that Proverb: "Length of days
in her right hand and in her left hand
riches and honor."

I'm not a palm reader, I'm a mother.

THE TAXI DRIVER

for Jessica

"I think of good ideas for stories," she said, blue
eyes glistening. "The girl pressed her face up
against the window, pig-nosed. And the taxi swerved."
There was more but it floated away like unheeded music
from a distant window. I watched her pretty features as they responded
to the fire of her imagination, remembered
her as an infant. I memorized her small face, her straight nose
and cleft chin with its teeny white blotches, when the doctor
laid her on my chest. I didn't want her stolen
away from me in the hospital. She was mine, and I would guard
her jealously with the image engraved on my mind.

"So the taxi driver changes," she finished. Pleased, she
lifted the fork with a flourish, speared her last bite of meat
from the emptied plate. I praised her creativity,
that sly thief taking her from me, snatching her from my arms,
from this home and our cozy dinners
even as I watched. There was no helping time,
the taxi driver would change
stories would bubble up for expression
and the music would keep playing
spilling out the window of that other house
to which she would eventually go.
All the images in the world couldn't save me.

GAYATRI MANTRA

for Madeleine

Hear, earth, sky, ether:

She was the miracle baby, the one
who wasn't supposed to be born
took seed anyway in my creaky 40 year old body like the sun
that hums across fibers of life
and lattices the many worlds
into being.
I meditate on her sacred effulgence
her laughing, squealing baby Buddha body
plump, wondrous and kissable
even as I change diapers, wipe vomit, and rub cocoa butter
and almond oil into wavy new stretch marks.

Radiant geometry stimulates us
when we chant it repetitively. But it's not the architecture
of light that makes the Divine accessible
immediate, intimate. It's the muddy incarnations
that bring that lesson home.

VALLEY OF THE BUTTERFLIES,
Petaloudes, Paros

The Greeks, having invented civilization, don't
cotton to service. Even at a luxury hotel
we were misguided, misdirected, misinformed.
Not an easy situation for impatient Americans
traveling with two young children.
I was seized one day with the eureka notion
of leaving the postcard-perfect port and pristine beach
for an excursion.
My husband was less enthused.
Our sun-drunk girls were blasé.

"Horsie, mommy," the little one said, clutching the post
of the wooden saddle frame on our steed.
"Donkey, baby."
"Horsie, mommy," she insisted. I let it be.
The better part of child-rearing is knowing which battles to wage.
Anyway, I was too busy laughing at her older sister
whose sprightly mount trotted indiscriminately
provoking a patter of vainglorious directives:
"No donkey, good donkey, whoa donkey, slow down,
Ohi, ohi, donkey, stop!"
The mangy beast carrying my husband
stopped to graze every few feet
for which she was roundly switched
by the wheezing grandfather guide
who hopped atop my donkey's rump
and masticated a cigarette stub
as he cursed her in Greek.
I didn't need to speak the language
to fathom its invective.
That was one ass whose parentage

was seriously in question.
"Horsie, mommy."
"Donkey, baby."
"*Ohi*, stop running, donkey, slow down!"
"Hey, don't leave me behind!"

This continued for kilometers
while we jounced our way through vineyards and farmlands
up a dirt path and over pebbly brown mountains
that gazed across the sea at Antiparos
the island across from this one
in the way that things always provoke their opposite.
It was all worth it when we dismounted
and not just because our bottoms hurt.
We clambered down a narrow path
into labyrinthine ivy groves flecked
with chocolate-winged creatures
a universe of them
who burst into red splendor when they ascended.
The little one poked with delight
her chubby fingers stroking the brown-striped
moths until they soared upward
and revealed their implicate, enfolded passion.

"Don't touch," admonished the ubiquitous German tourists.
"Can't you read the signs?"
But I didn't care. Whatever flutters
of discomfort she caused them,
those beings of change and glory,
were redeemed by what continued in our imagination
long after the pain in our saddle-sore limbs subsided
(Which was long enough).

TIGER IN THE GARDEN

There are tigers in the garden
round my baby's crib
I chew on my heart with my fear

They are orange and black
and invincible
they float on obscure breezes
like lethal muscled butterflies
we bred them as dream-cubs
I nursed them with a bottle
a big pink nipple
Now they have turned against us

A chain-link fence circumscribes the flowers
Marigolds and black roses
creeping purple phlox
I must take the baby out
flee the tigers
who don't know pity or love
who would rend my baby's body
scoop out her entrails
tear out her tongue
bloody smears on the bushes

No one hears me, no one believes me
my eyeballs have withered
in their sockets
my lungs are desiccated

crumbling dry leaves in my chest
my throat is charred
the baby is crying

There are tigers in the garden
round my baby's crib
They are prowling on the perimeter
waiting, waiting
watching

ICE PACKS

Children learn to soothe themselves
by attaching to something
soft, cuddlesome, a blanket or bunny
that recalls mommy
her starry omniscient breath
the joyful ground of being that is her bosom,
her sweet accessible
touch on their satiny skin
I've watched my toddlers stroke the silky
edge of their blankey's
eyes dissolving
limbs liquescent until they doze
but this after
they've stroked my lips
as nursing babies.

You exercise with a vengeance and then ice
your knee, the pain justifies
for you the time to fuss over yourself
to put up your feet and caress
yourself. Your mother,
locked away as she is
now in an institution somewhere
surely could not bear your tiny fingers
on her mouth, that door
into the deepest and most hidden
needs of the self that will not
be denied.
So you rub your ice packs
and are lulled, somewhere within you
a baby is crying and her tears
are met with frozen silence.

SWEET MOTHER

There are moments when ecstasy descends, a play of light
Delicious down the ladder from heaven, the double helix.
Sri Aurobindo speaks of cellular transformation, so eloquent,

His authority in the Mother absolute, I know Her too
In my bones and my breath, the fragmenting echo of a mantra
In those moments when ecstasy descends and plays with light.

The opening is complete, through the irises, through the pores
Washed by blood into the organelles. Even the electrons dance
When Sri Aurobindo speaks of cellular transformation. So eloquent

Is bliss that surrender becomes the goal, that thing I have eluded
All my life, stretched thin between the fleeing and the waiting
For that one moment that ecstasy descends for me to play with light

That originates and climaxes in mystery. I shatter into the void—
Selfless presence—Her intimacy too big to hold the valence as
Sri Aurobindo speaks of the cellular. Transformation is so eloquent,

Molding in the scattered plasticity of my flesh a form for soul,
Muscles shuddering, ripping, to birth me into the embodiment
Of those moments. So ecstasy descends. In a play of light
Sri Aurobindo speaks: Cellular transformation is so eloquent.

MY DADDY'S THUMB

As a girl I used to stare
at it
the glowering ropey scar
behind your nail
where once
like everyone else
you had wholeness:
a thumbtip.
Each time I asked, you
told a different story,
there were so many of them.
Sometimes it was a hunting accident,
the cunning slip of a knife while
skinning a white-tail deer
disgorging a pheasant
disemboweling a green and iridescent mallard
on a cold morning in a reed-bound blind,
which left me with a queasy
instinct about your pet
name for me: 'Duck.'
Or it was on the Michigan farm
where you were raised by a strict man
who was not your father
that you hacked off
a piece of yourself.
Another time it was a baseball story,
you played
for the Chicago minors, or was that
just another tale to bolster
what remained
of your pride
after booze had tattered it?

You died of lung cancer.
When your mind succumbed
to metastasis
they went to get you,
stacks of red cigarette boxes
fell out the door, dozens
and dozens. There wouldn't be enough,
you feared,
you who had surfeit graven
into your hand, so in those last few weeks
you scoured the Navy Exchange
with a fever to fill
your insufficiency.

After you passed, I saw
you, the gift and the curse
of a second sight.
'Come,' you beckoned
'Come to me here.
Join me
it will be different
now. I am different.'
But you wavered like distant heat
in the vague blue bardos
laughing while I said kaddish
having instructed in a will
that left everything to your
other daughter
that you be cremated.
So I returned to my prayers
praising God the creator of a bountiful earth
laying to rest my fantasies
of a daddy
whose hand
like his soul
was unscathed.

DECONSTRUCTING THE ASTROLOGY OF LOVE

His Mars trines my Venus, that's a happy angle
like when I used to get cosines and arcsines
right on trig tests back in high school, the teacher
was pleased and so was I, transference functioning
at its Oedipal best. His Moon, that's 'Mom' in star lexicon
sits on the mask of my rising sign—Libra in my horoscope—
a vacillating constellation but inclined to prettiness
and pleasant enough if you don't mind arguing
every other hour, especially over art. My Uranus
like a daft spark plug zaps his trollopy Venus,
electricity galore and anyway, who said eros was supposed
to be comfortable? Our Sun's square off
at each other, with Pluto smoldering in there
like a nuclear power plant gone into meltdown,
the whole configuration forcing the issue of self-
expression and individuation, but what's relationship without
conflagration, as if we needed a sacred science
to tell us what the heart knows without metaphor,
what neither word nor symbol can signify as love,
what tender Presence redeems the void beyond meaning.

PUTS & CALLS

for Jon

I have never been attracted to artists, those heathen
with their infernal torn jeans and their profanely
frayed savings accounts. Destitution isn't redeemed by indwelling
sexiness at least for me. I've smashed the idol of poverty
within myself, venerating nameless
Abundance with the diverse devotional characters
inhabiting my psyche, righteous as they are.
The banker's blue wool and burgandy tie
invoke my worshipful response.
Even in our most godless moments of hostility
and what marriage doesn't at times forsake its faith
I have always revered in my husband
The Businessman.

We dine out with our friends, she the stock analyst
he the lawyer, they talk about options the butterfly
spread profiting from the volatility the rippling chi
inherent in that holy face of divinity
the Stock Market, blessed be It.
My husband's mind races gracefully through statistical formula
like a calculator and dollar signs flash ka-chink
ka-chink in his eyes. I listen in juicy devout silence,
it is lyrical to me. We come home
and when at last our children
those costly and inquisitive beasts
are asleep, I call
to my husband, Put
your suit back on, I am in the mood
to pray.
He says, Okay, and you put
on that little maid's outfit
and high heels and do you mind if I videotape
our devotions?

ORACLE

There's no end to augury.
Years ago a seer told me: "You were
one of those at Delphi. Craggy and mountainous,
the earth's navel, prophecy, celibacy. It was hard for you.
A curly-haired man came, you fled with him.
You sailed to Creta, lived contented,
children and animal husbandry,
a kindly community,
but in fear of being found.
Reprisal was death,
stony and slow."

This is a story
about love, and therefore about betrayal
and anguish.
The heart lives in dialectic. This is a story
of making a choice, and living
and dying
with the consequences,
a tale of what it means
to be human. We never take on flesh
without also taking on cruelty.
And, like any good soap opera, the story repeats.

Flashbacks comment
on the present, and visions of
the past and future describe what is now:
More love, betrayal, anguish.
Another choice.
Characters differ, point-of-view remains the same,
crisis recurs,

outcome varies in increments of sorrow and bliss
but will end again
to begin again.

It can only be redeemed
when I someday shuck off bodies for good
and meet the Witness
to this unfolding who might tell me:
*"There is no reprisal. All was illusion
except the love. In every plot line you lived
out both choices. Do you not continue
as I do, in my image,
timeless and creative?"*

But the moment is opaque,
access to the Witness obstructed
by centuries of amnesiac struggle
to return to that virginal prophetic center
that once abandoned
was not reclaimed
by integration.
So I seek out soothsayers
as perhaps a curly-haired man sought me out
millennia ago
and left with a wife
who had cast off her prerogatives
with her inviolability
and would live again to claim her fullness.

Revelation and repetition compulsion are sacred twins;
we're always trying to get things right
another time around.

VIRGIN

Consecration is what you make of it.
The other night I tendered a blessing
To an unsuspecting man, my body,
Sensation and soul, proved the vessel.

In the old days I was a priestess
Raised in service to the Goddess, I am
Possessed of clear memories of my vestal duties:
Make love only once to a man
Who came alone to the white temple seeking
Her bounty
Instead of making love to only one man
During a life of service to him alone.

An Intercontinental dwelling, a luxury
After a day of teaching with my hands.
Late night tea and an invitation
To explore the perfect shoulders, thinning
Hair, the lithe legs of a man who venerates
His body at the gym.

I wove his shakti up through the shushumma
Thrummed his root to the pulse of earth
Coaxed open the tube at the lotus point
Where heaven descends through the crown
To seed the flesh with spirit.
The flow is down through woman,
Up through man, counterintuitive
But effective. He was a wholer man
When I left him, and I pleased
To find the ancient skills intact.

To remember was the after sacrament,
Read responsively with forgetting,
Like two asanas always paired
To right the body during union.
The necessary vespers ensued
For a married lady and mom
To tell herself it was all in a day's work:
The liturgical lay.

PONN FARR

"A thing of beauty is always a disturbance."
  Mr. *Spock,* Star Trek

On the corner of 83rd and Amsterdam
there stands a man hailing a taxi
on weekday mornings when I go to the gym.
He is dark-haired, coal-eyed,
roughly made like a hasty carving
in a reluctant medium,
and deliciously pin-striped,
a grey wool overcoat flung over his shoulders,
unbuttoned. I want him.
I have imagined taking him
into some small third-floor apartment
with a futon in the corner and ivy
in the window, my fingers on his white collar,
his large hands on my belly,
the alacrity of longing and submission,
an incandescent anonymity.

After the glaciation, the last seven years
frost of this difficult marriage
to which I am tied by debt and affection,
I welcome the throb beneath my navel
the slow burn like an alchemist's
fire in my pelvis, this indiscriminate
support for the whole structure,
and the loamy slack ease of my thighs
parting in reverie.

It isn't necessary to approach
him. The real and the unreal
twine about me, one cool indivisible river
out of which pokes my head like an errant

stone. This time will pass too. The long cycles
of a long marriage
follow their own immutable logic,
however they restrain
my passions in all but fantasy.
Discipline yields its own rewards. Disturbances
like all beautiful things fade
and what is left is time.

ICON

You are beautiful. In other lives
You were my lover. A woman then
Buttery moon breasts, long white legs
I remember the down sloping along the curve
Of the soft flesh giftwrapped around your femur.

Now you are a man, I a woman, the beloved
Polarity I have spiraled myself around
These many lifetimes as a priestess
A nun, a monk, and a whore, to the householder
Now incised with inconsequent memories.

We will never meet. Locality is irrelevant.
I have already tongued the dimple of your iliac
Spine, smelled the husky salt
Scent of your man's perineum. All this
Because of aurochs and angels, prophetic
Sonnets, enduring recall, the failure
Of art to offer refuge from all that pulses
In the hallowed space where artifice
Ends and the heart begins.
So the heart begins,
And it begins,
Again.

PAGAN

Ungodly
this thirst for you
and not your soul, either,
though I'm happy to possess that, too.
It's your sculpted chest
the waist as lean and lithe as a little girl's
the muscled thighs and the fisted oak
that is anything but feminine
rising from between them.
I suck you in
all my fierceness sluicing out around you
I lie underneath, dominating us
both with my boneless surrender
and fluid carnal rage.
I am a river and you raft me
I am a nymph and you ravish me
I am the night and you shatter me
with light that penetrates
everywhere, nothing is exempt
I am that thing that yields and moans
that soft thing that is feared and desired
but so little understood
You can own me, control me, grasp me,
assault me with pleasure and still find
I have been free all along

ARTIST

for Sabin

does the stone feel the first chip of the adze
or clay respond to the first thrill of fingers
shaping it to some higher purpose? I like to think
they do, that even a wash of color
quivers at the approach of a brush
and the exquisite pain of that intent
to saturate some blank space
with a hue spread to ravishment.

form is the sculptor's prerogative
and surrender the final recourse.
only love could make it so,
demand it so,
speak it into being amidst the dross
and shavings that some wind
will shiffle off into nothingness.

Rejoice, beloved,
that the lover handles you
with such shattering craftsmanship.
were it not for you, your sweetness,
your beauty, I too
would struggle against the creator's hand.
knowing you, I know in ecstasy
what otherwise is the nihilist's cry:
we are all raw material for His using.

IN ITALY, MANNEQUINS HAVE NIPPLES

He was a miser, stank, wore his leather boots to bed
asked to be buried in his spurs. He was gay
but wrote poetry to a Christian lady, argued
with popes, was canny and faked
paintings in the hand of Older Masters.
He had excellent PR. His surly temper
precluded many friends, but Raphael
sneaked into the Sistine Chapel to be raptured
by his art. Indeed, who is not? Buonarroti
depicted himself flayed, but in Christ's line of sight.
The rest of us transcend our skins
when caught up in the spectacle of his Judgment
Day, or the eyes of the Delphic oracle.

Walking along the Via Condotti, rich dresses dazzle me, wrapped
around vivacious Roman women and shameless
sexy plastic forms. Seduction
like a good house wine intoxicates
me. I want a man in my arms
and I want grace's dispensation.
There is an empty pad of paper by my bed.
It is clear that my art, fueled by ferocious longing,
will not bring me the release I pray for. In this
I keep the company of my betters. Matter is a haloed thief
of spirit. The body begets unredeemed light.

TRIPTYCH PLUS ONE

after Rumi

APPLE OF MY EYE
It's that time again. AM, PM,
A quarter past; I am alone again
In a bed that aches for your sinful gravity
As I do:
    Let me lie down beneath you, love,
    And be the earth to your fall.

INCANTATORY INCARNATIONS
"Sister and brother, lovers, mother and child
You have been every karmic dyad possible
in the heliacal dance of your past lives"
intoned the mystic. I was glad to hear
We'd been destined together for seventy thousand years.
It's the last thirty apart that have spellbound me into eternity.

CLAIRAUDIENCE
At every moment, I hear your soul note. I listen invasively.
You respond to my encroaching attention,
Like a moth flying closer into the veil of light
That will inflame its being. It is the flame's sweetest purpose
To consume with love
And the moth's tenderest ultimatum.

NON-LOCAL SPECTRA
What is real in this private exchange
effected in our souls' vestibules?
Do houses need to abut to create neighbors?
Isn't it enough that a small dwelling
can sit on the prairie beneath the plenum of space
and resonate to its foundations
with a city apartment?
    The lover knows immediately what the scientist pieced together
    painstakingly after centuries:
    Distance vanishes before the merging.

THE ARTHUR MURRAY LOVER

for Charlie

In my dreams I dance
with you, slow slow, quick quick, I
sway to your magic step like a vine
on a trellis, turn in conversation
your pale cheek pressed against my darker one
my palm curved around your strong-boned shoulder
as familiar as only sleep remembers.
We swing, step, in a teak-floored room
crowded with faces I no longer know
and the wall mirrors watch as I go
after you, chase, those wide brown eyes
flirting, and I move to close
into your arms. Sunlight—dissolution
repeats itself—the white mists twinkle
under my lids, and I spin, stumble.
into all the redoubled absence.

THE SECRET,
WILLIAM BOUGUEREAU, 1875

There is that play between innocence and what it is
Not, realistically. Two sweet-faced girls and a blue scarf
knotted around the pretty pink marble throat
of one who is listening, listening
to that which can not be repeated. An upraised
finger, lithe and blush, in the photo-idealism
of the artist's distinguishing style, the adorable
digit pointing to lead the eye away from the hidden
thing—a message, a cipher, God's word made manifest?—the fleshy cherub
drafts in the sly surface
of the well.
    I keep the painting in my bedroom
which has something to say of carnality.
It's second generation art, an oil rendered by a lesser
painter, my unknown contemporary, in homage. Still,
perhaps *The Secret* will redeem this room
with all its perjured sweetness and clandestine
sensuality. After all,
what is allegory but illusion with airs?

CRUCIFEROUS VEGETABLES

I no longer eat meat. I sacrificed coffee
Years ago, when I began the training
To be a healer. The demands of my energy
System, I am always explaining,
Have required that I concentrate on broccoli,
Chard, carrots and cauliflower, that most
Peaceable of vegetables. Spaghetti
Squash, when put in the oven to roast,
Makes a delicious and sacred accompaniment
To any meal. Sugar is next to excise
From my diet, which is only a condiment
To the sumptuous feast of my spiritual practice.
It is all to live with greater mindfulness of the God Within
Who after all made chocolate vegetarian.

DOMESTICATED BEASTS

> "... and so Pygmalion
> Marvels, and loves the body he had fashioned."
> Ovid, Metamorphosis

The Poem-Dog
I put it in motion, then
it stuck its head out the window
ears cocked, and a passing car scraped
its nose off. A new one grew.

The Poem-Cat
Cats pincer cockroaches
in their mouths, and leave
carcasses as gifts on the bed. Bare
green guts ooze on striped sheets.
Sometimes after dark they coalesce
back into the body, innards
taking on the cracked carapace.

The Poem-Gerbil
Its tail twisted off in my hand
after I chased it around the house and through the nave of the cherry desk.
It skittered past. I grabbed.
Later, as I rubbed out the speckles of blood,
the tail grew a one-armed gerbil.
This gerbil couldn't run.

The Poem-Garter-Snake
This one wasn't supposed to be
there, hiding behind the rusty
sink in the cellar. It
Blinked. Sss!
If I slashed off--
would new ones bloom?

REVELATIONS

for Rita

I had the presence of mind to become
a self-hating Jew
shortly after conversion
that stripping away of my old Self's identity
which lent authenticity
to the experience. I pondered
this making the ritual kugel for the Seder
in my mother-in-law's house.
She stood at another counter molding
matzoh balls while the chicken soup simmered
golden and luscious with sweet dillweed for garnish
chopped into a glass bowl
and the brisket which still-vegetarian I do not eat,
clutching a scrap of my Lenten past, roasted
in garlic juice with yellow onions and celery at 325°. There were
asparagus cut into pretty bright pieces
and boxes of Passover chocolate stacked by the refrigerator.
My honey-brown-haired little daughter napped upstairs
curled into the soft part of my husband's belly
my blue-eyed big daughter inked up a manilla pad
with pictures of houses, rainbows, and talking animals
and waited for her cousins
those children of an upbringing alien to mine
to arrive.
I wanted to but I didn't curse
when I scraped a chunk of skin off my knuckle
along with a potato peeling.
Instead I held up my hand and watched
the blood run. "It's real kugel now,"
my mother-in-law said, "with a little
knuckle juice grated in."

God is, the red river explained as I stared,
and has many faces. Life and consciousness
are forever flowing into new forms.
Change is.
A few weeks had elapsed since the clear passion of Easter
which I no longer celebrate
and a few fond years were yet to pass
before the marriage disintegrated utterly
but it was still a resurrection
a moment of freedom to be commemorated
with wine and questions
and an egg laid out on the Seder plate
a moment of atonement to remember the sacrifice
that took place in the old Temple
which like all cherished structures
shatters to release new life.

HEAVEN'S GATE

after the cult's mass suicide in March, 1997

Shrieking mutawiyyin flog women
those lewdest of possessions
for exposing an ankle.
Hasidim with their long curls
tzitzit peeking out beneath
quaint nineteenth century attire
band together against the world
marry only their own kind
mate through holes in the sheets
and refuse to count a woman in a prayer quorum.
An orthodox rabbi won't even touch a woman
won't share the meagerest gesture
the godly gift of human contact
because she might be unclean.
The Christian right preaches the One
way, the True way and no Man cometh
to the Father except by way of Me, the Son,
the Only way. Buddhists ignore
this world, as if non-attachment
that ultimate narcissism
could truly release all sentient beings
from their suffering. What is a cult
but the sentimental histrionics of a media
television, newspapers, radio, magazines
who ought to get down on their knees
and thank the poor delusional prophet
a twisted and ungrounded channel
who sent a thirsty, misguided crew
into purple shrouds and UFO's.
Without such shrill condemnation
their profits would be poorer.

Compared to the atrocities
we all commit daily
in desperate hopes of battering down
heaven's gates,
suicide is such a small thing.
It is the castration that seals the judgment,
the ancient fear of the feminine,
unknown life arising out of the uncontrollably
fecund void: Here come the witches,
and they're gonna chop off balls.

BLUES, GRAYS & BIG-HEAD WHITES

From all over the multiverse
they come
to study earth, create
shimmering borealis showers above credible
but incredulous viewers
play tag with 747's
pluck time from local lines
carve niches into livestock
and worse, abduct the innocent
evaluate
impregnate.
Can't they think of anything
more original
than to mirror our mythic
fears so precisely?

We are not alone. From the Vedic
vimanas to Ezekial's chariot
Quetzalcoatl's raft of serpents
Ra's barge
the Sumerian Anunnaki, those who from heaven
to earth came
to fornicate with the daughters of Earth

I don't need UFO's to teach
me what I can learn from the mirror.
I see the ET in myself:
head too large, eyes too
big, neck too long, mouth small
God is there but so too
is the image of my alienation.

Through these lolling worlds
from the electron to the galaxy
colliding dimensions, ricocheting realities
light refracting countless times
we perceive something greater
even than the form of God:

Divine mirth.

THE KAMA SUTRA/TORAH

The book quantifies
interlaced limbs, sumptuous
robes, ideal positions, heavenly countenances
robust appendages even God
would be proud to claim

I read and wonder
deer, mare or elephant
to what class of woman
do I belong, have I mastered
enough of the graceful arts
and am I limber enough
to do it this way, or that
Not to mention the 10 commandments
the 613 mitzvot proliferating
through millennia and gray-bearded debate
like spotted toadstools in decaying moss
into another magnitude of law
more baroque even than the rapture
of St. Teresa

I am still counting. I've done this,
I've done that, I put my fist inside myself
to gauge my animal nature
Soon the numbers distend, bleed out
of shape, squirm like eviscerated
mealworms.
I shall inscribe
a new vulgate, and bind it on my children
on our foreheads and our hands
and our bellies and our thighs

on lingam and yoni
It won't be enough, some cells
will still escape the silken cords that secure
the lover's wrists

Adonai and Shiva elude embrace
Shekhinah and Shakti obliterate words
Love exculpates Kali Yuga
    Codification
        hot damp white rotting flowers
        fails beneath God's breath

STORIES FOR VLADIMIR

I don't like your writing, you say,
your dark Russian eyebrows like God's
thunderclouds punctuating
your speech. Then you kiss me.
You ask,
Would you sleep with me
and my wife?
Of a man less beautiful, less brilliant
less sure of himself—
the immigrant Jew who started as a janitor
obtained a Harvard MBA
and made a fortune on Wall Street
before he was 40—
it would be comical
this exquisite devastation
that ensues from so complete an iconoclasm
of my cherished graven images.
Is it that I am tempted to collude (my old pattern)
or appalled?
I will make you like my psalms,
I will write pornography for you,
what kind of story would you like,
tell me, I put my palms on your thighs
at the same time
leaning toward and away from you.
You talk about such sexy things, you say,
I am so aroused.

Later I wonder what it is about my energy
that magnetizes such offers to me
with a bleak and humorous regularity
and I scold myself
for any lurking complicity
as if idolatrous I
hadn't been waiting for that soft certain kiss
for so long
like a resurrection from the dead.

GANESHA

for Loren Eiseley

Elephantine grace
I have seen you
dancing where boulders are strewn
across the ocher altiplano
the lunar-like scratch pad
for animal glyphs
lasting symbols of evanescence
spied like mind's perimeters
only from a flight above

I have watched you
playing across miles and miles of lines
Peru and Percival Lowell's canals
the immense journey time takes
from animalcule to globular cluster
singing where oil slicks suck down children

I have observed you
riding their small skeletons
sere eyes and sweet bones flayed
into the secret pits of Kansas wheat fields
golden and swaying and murmuring
the ancient language of logos
wind, loam, the prairie's extension into cosmos
out past the sticky blue nebulae
new stars tearing holes in matter's womb
milky way sockets in the bison's skull

I have witnessed you
spinning galaxies across infinity's dialectic
the Universe is a violent place

there can be no discussion without
articulating suffering
evoluting and longing

I have felt you
your gray trunk
rasping on my neck, my ribs, my feet
that epochs ago were fin and claw
an eon from now spent in the alembic of life
will morph at will between light and substance
now stumbling flesh over sinastral tropes

There is no end to imagination
no limit to the tongue's obstacles
only heart, psalming and soaring.
We bolt ourselves against God
Whose promises efface the soul's plains
Your work is never done
Your play weaves life together
Your song chords the world
Your word incarnates dilemma
Wisdom and the cycles of unknowing

Ganesha:
unburden me

THE BEAR MAN

for D.

You wear a garland of shells whose sea
clatter is silenced by your voice speaking stories and compassions
and from out of the Zen gap
the death of your wife who was your ground of being
arises like stars from the womb of a nebula
that one necessary thing that observes itself.

Your eyes are full of black moon totems
tall and carved faces, some grinning, some bleak
they are not punctual because lines melt
into ellipses that lead away from the truth
and the journey is incomparable
referencing only itself and the God who arches over it.

Your hands hold a knife to illumine the knotted
way, its hilt pearled over with patterns of growth
whose tidal flux is best tracked by following the footsteps of the dark
beast, the one without a name that can be uttered aloud.
There is a hooded figure within and it is in the grappling
that the reluctant angel tenders a blessing.

Shaman, trickster, counselor: you sit in motion
in the place where all the realms come together, ask
questions and deflect answers, leave a greater space
and clearer mystery where certainty choked
the flow. It is in unknowing, unlearning, unburdening,
that healing happens, and the soul grows whole.

REFLECTIONS FROM THE TWELFTH HOUSE

for D.H.

You are a pearl in full luster
of nacre gleaming and bright
whose surface you use to show
others their faces. "Be careful,"
I admonish, "you will attract
narcissists." "What a perceptive
observation," you answer.

We are old friends. I have enjoyed
your richness, the sparkle
between us. You comment on what is
elusive about me, but you never invade.
I have cherished the sanctity
of my retiring spaces
been allowed in our intertwinings
the rare and precious
gift of my solitude with my love.

My moon lives in a house of *moksha*.
It is the worst of the *dusthanas*, the evil
or harmful abodes. It is true
there has been suffering
but what gem is created without pressure?
When final liberation is at stake
there are allowances to be made.
There is still mutual reception
between luminaries
as between old friends
a kind of acceptance
which always mitigates. It is a higher yoga
a rare union of comfort
with the brilliance of soul.

BATHSHEBA

Splashing pale water on her arms and breasts,
Does she know that he is watching? Her beauty tests
The psalmist, whose gaze dews over her limbs with a curse
Of lust that will dissolve his family. First
The death of their first born son, no passing over
For the house of David. The sister's lover
Her brother whose affection gushes into hate:
Betrayal, rape, public acrimony. It is original sin, and fate
That next sweeps the beautiful son into a tangled tree.
                                                    Awareness
Streams forth, a protean consciousness
Of I and thou sluicing through the body's gullies: the tidal
Quantum pull of being beheld creates the watcher. The bridal
Bath has manifest her, form and flesh. She is guilty, as we are,
Of responding when God perceives us from afar.

KING LEAR

... Love's not love
When it is mingled with regards that stands
Aloof from the entire point.   (I.i.238-240)

We take our mythologies from different plays.
I am Cordelia
who has only her love to give
and mute before a treacherous sister,
betrayal and invalidation
enacted in scene
after scene in my life.
Those closest to me
loved best by me
have always done me wrong.
You are Petruchio
who tamed his Kate
with love that begets love
won the one true mate
good enough reason
to stay married to your dead wife.
These are not truths but only
fables that mediate
the thing itself
the rose-colored, gossamer and steel
essential thing that arcs from heart
to heart. Which of us
you with your happy trope
me with my rueful one
is more authentic?
Is there any honesty in metaphor?

What bridge spans the distance,
a living vine or rainbow seine of iambic pentameter,
is built less on truth
than on fictions
we are willing to set aside.

THE CATHEDRAL AT COLOGNE

It took 800 years to complete. Vaulting
into the sky, stretched thin between earth
and heaven. Centuries of labor, sacrifice, commitment.
I am talking about the human
heart, the time required to build an edifice
of love. I am talking about intimacy.
I am talking about how we are all scored with pain.
Some of those wounds are vertical,
deep cuts leading us upward,
but it is the horizontal brokenness we don't see
that sanctifies our faith in one another.

I stood watching my husband, that militant Jew,
light a candle and chant the shehechiyanu,
thanking G-d for this moment. He bent
over his pocket to count the marks
into the offertory. He whispered a plea
he thought I didn't hear
"Protect our children, Adonai, and let this marriage
survive." He prayed in this city
of pogroms.
He prayed in the cathedral
that lacks a rose window
for fear of distracting the eye
from its celestial ascent
as if crosshatching
wasn't God's handwriting.

And I turned away with tears
knowing that faith itself is sometimes inadequate
forgiveness belated
and redemption a spire lost in clouds.
If heaven hears us, it is when we merge our differences
and geometry
like all broken vows
expires.

THE ROAD AFTER DAMASCUS

Since then I have shed friends and family and lost a husband.
They have been peeled off like layers of skin
by an acid. What remains underneath is sometimes
charred, sometimes new. I drop pieces of myself
along the way like a mad leper
pleading to be healed
repulsed by my own ugliness
fascinated by how little can adhere
and still leave me alive, traveling.
I have interrogated Gospels, Mishna, Vedas, myths
thrown the I-Ching
scanned the hooded eyes of gypsy tarot readers
badgered the sky to reveal itself
chewed on old poetry and new
even hunkered down with new age pulp.

I asked for this, two decades ago
kneeling in the salt marsh
of an estuary where swans mate in the spring
and bluefish run in August,
felt the hand of God in the foggy stillness
my teenaged heart arching into the bliss of that palm
that cradles the world in the indigo void.
I asked in innocence, in the juvenile
expectation that revelation occurs daily
like egg sandwiches at lunch
that immanence is not this inquisitive trudging
into the covert ignorance, darkness, despair
I do not wish to acknowledge
as riddling my core.

Even before birth I practiced.
The bright light, the blindness, the voice
exhorting me to faith, the new name,
all stock characters played in new venues
like a ragtag troupe clowning down the receding road
of the commedia dell'arte.
The pattern of the plot persists: go forth,
get lost, slay the fire-breathing ego,
sacrifice whatever it is that matters most,
then the prize: grace, followed by
return. I am still disintegrating.

I am still waiting. I am still
traveling. I have arrived
at the meager knowledge only
that the road itself is divine, the journey
is sacrament, and enlightenment
is every echoing footstep along the way.

PRAYER

Quan Yen of a thousand compassionate
Ears, a thousand soft hands,
Who has filled the bellies
Of women weeping for child
Or food for their daughters
Swaying in step not yet burdened
By anomie and accommodation, that accidental
Atrophying of age
Who has cradled in their hearts
Hope for their muscular sons ascending
On disentangled threads of light
To still pastures flocked with lambent awe
From fields of war exhausted with gore

Quan Yen, Quan Yen, I shout
Your name, the sound wafts
Like Cain's smoke toward your
Boddhisattva sanctuary, through the meager
Song of myself, so few measures there,
Past the glass sphere
That entraps the denser earth
Fluttering through the last barrier
Do your ears hear beyond
The curving blue horizon, that unapologetic
Edge between everywhere
And dissolution of the final shape of God

All it takes is one
One ear
One hand
One moment

To answer—
Even some spastic indulgence—
My one
Plea
To rapture me
Flesh and soul
With my one
Love

BODY & PSALM

Praise drips from gashes on my fingertips
There is no bliss like mine
I have been worshiping the divine.
                            Ecumenical,
I bow, knees scraping shards of broken faiths,
Torn flesh, and then
And only then
Satiny oil on the slick of periosteum
All other space being unarticulated
Does the Goddess enter.

Who is She to demand such revelry? I
Dance nude and vomit when the goats with white fur
Charge up the mountain
To fly in all directions before me,
And what is left of the I
Who fancies itself
A brain, two brown eyes, functional ovaries
Breasts that softened after nursing three daughters?

But I give over to her, tearing at my palms
With my teeth, whispering the mantra
Mary, Astarte, Quan Yen, the name
Doesn't matter. Only the yielding.
Anything for grace.

THE ECLECTIC AGNOSTIC

Once I was Christian,
now I am Jewish, years
of meditation have distilled
within me a Buddhist
slant on things. Patanjali
explains that the experience
of the void catechizes one so.
Called
by some whimsical deity
to the healing profession, the laying
on of hands: *Ground,
Center, Open your heart*, went the litany
of my instruction,
I encountered Aphrodite, sea foam
flesh, in the subtle realms,
Aphrodite of the beautiful arms,
Pallas Athena, Kali, Lao Tzu, even Ezekial
Once. I have lately
Embodied a genteel pantheism.

Does it matter in what bed of the tongue
Matter inseminates spirit? We are all rushing
from the inferno,
from the unreal to the real,
from darkness into light,
fleeing from the knowledge
of our own immortality
into the voluptuous embrace of the fear
of death. Purify me, O Lord,
renew in me a right heart.
Kadosh, kadosh, kadosh.

IN MY NEXT LIFETIME

for Gerda

In my next lifetime, when I come back, I will ski more and worry less.
I will begin every dinner with dessert, and it will be dark chocolate,
or something gooey
and coconut.
I will choose dresses for color and not for whether or not they make
me look slim. I am thinking yellow,
purple, and butterfly prints
in chintz.
I will start using sunblock when I am 12, the same age
when I will begin practicing
yoga
because it makes me feel so peaceful and good.

In my next lifetime, when I come back, I will choose
a comfortable upper-middle-class family to host my wandering
soul. I've seen that great wealth imposes anxiety
and demands of its own. Too little to work for
ruins people. So does poverty, my old scourge.
The lack of money—for graduate school, for good doctors,
for guitar lessons, for the occasional porterhouse steak and soul-ravishing
trip to Paris—
is one of the great evils that besets humanity.

In my next lifetime, and I hope the Earth isn't ruined before
I make it back, I will play outside more, which can mean lying
on my back beneath an oak tree and reading something
luscious
like Dickens
or Yeats
or a cheesy romance novel. I will spend more time staring into the sky
and no time at all on a therapist's couch.

I will say
"Yes!"
more often and do the dishes only when they're piled up to the ceiling.
I will turn off the TV but go to every sci-fi movie
that opens. I will choose more friends who understand
that I'm originally from
the planet Xetron
and that this beautiful blue and green orb
is just a way station on my peregrinations. They will laugh more with me
than at me and they will understand the value of
spontaneous dance.
I have only a few of those kind in this life.
I miss them all the time.

In my next lifetime, since
I'm not enlightened
and I will have to return to complete the balance
I will say "I love you" to the people I love:
on the hour, every hour. Even when I hate them.
And especially when they hate me.

In my next lifetime I will be
the luminous me
I always wanted to be now, and somehow fell short of.
It wasn't for the absence of an open heart or effort.
Rather, I tried too hard, and let gravity weigh
me down. So in my next life, I will let my
open heart lift, and shine me to everyone I meet.

SEVA

was it the tanned young
man browsing the racks
the kind
you wanted to throw
a leg over
and ride real hard
when he modeled the sports coat
for me and smiled
"Buy this one
for your husband,
the cloth is fine"

or was it the honeysuckle leaves
emerald tendrils
of light extruding
toward me
as I jogged
to the beach, three
point four miles
on a summer's
evening, warm
and lucent
on my clavicles
as I panted
in the salty damp

was it the kettle pond
on the Cape
soft froggy fresh water
abandoned
by the receding
glacier, lily pads
and fish bubbles
I floated facing

up to the mirroring
sky
I floated near
the edge where willow
fingers flicked in
to scatter the dragonflies
or was it the swelling
of ancient chants
at the ashram

all the wounded folk
who can not rectify
themselves apart
from prescribed diurnal
devotions
longing for salvation
like me
as if the guru
in all her obliterating
magnificence
could incarnate
outside our own
hearts, skins
the eye
I
within

I have been waiting a lifetime
to know
so
what was it
that taught me
finally that every
body, every
thing
the whole Earth
its greedy fullness
is performing a service
simply by being

ACKNOWLEDGEMENTS

THE MOUNTAIN ASTROLOGER: "Deconstructing the Astrology of Love" (Oct/Nov 1999).
KARAMU: "The Cathedral" (Vol. XVII, No. 2, Spring 2001).
OREGON EAST MAGAZINE: "Atzilut & Asiyah" (Volume XXXI, September 2000).
LUMINA: "My Daddy's Thumb" (Volume VI, Fall, 2000).
PMS (poem/memoir/story): "One Weekend in the Astral Plane" (Number 1, Spring, 2001).
LICKING RIVER REVIEW: "The Eclectic Agnostic" and "Artist" (Volume 32, Summer, 2001).
CONFLUENCE: "Oracle" (Volume 12, 2001).
FOX CRY REVIEW: "Virgin" (Volume 27, September 2001).
ECLIPSE: "Pagan" (Spring, 2002).
WIND: "The Cathedral at Cologne, February 2001" (Issue 86, Winter 2001-2002).
LIMESTONE: "My Children's Arms" and "Stories for Vladimir" (Fall, 2003).
PENNSYLVANIA ENGLISH: "Bathsheba" (Fall, 2003).
ELM The Eureka Literary Review: "The Taxi Driver" (Spring, 2004).
THE SOUTH CAROLINA REVIEW: "The Kama Sutra/Torah" (Spring, 2005).
SULPHUR RIVER LITERARY REVIEW: "In Italy, Mannequins Have Nipples" (Volume XXI, No. 2, Fall, 2005).
RIVER'S EDGE: "Spirit Houses" (Volume XVIII, No. 1, Spring, 2005).

www.ingramcontent.com/pod-product-compliance
Lightning Source LLC
Chambersburg PA
CBHW031415040426
42444CB00005B/581